S0-HIP-998

The Cross Bearing of a Pastor's Wife

by

Dr. Deloise C. Thorne

xulon PRESS

NOV 2 6 2010

Copyright © 2010 by Dr. Deloise C. Thorne

The Cross Bearing of a Pastor's Wife
by Dr. Deloise C. Thorne

Printed in the United States of America

ISBN 9781609574680

All rights reserved solely by the author. The author guarantees all contents are original and do not infringe upon the legal rights of any other person or work. No part of this book may be reproduced in any form without the permission of the author. The views expressed in this book are not necessarily those of the publisher.

Unless otherwise indicated, Bible quotations are taken from The King James Version Bible. Copyright © 1988 by B.B. Kirkbride Bible Co., Inc. Indianapolis, Indiana; and The New Century Version Bible. Copyright © 1996 by Word Publishing.

Word definitions are taken from the dictionary software WordWeb 2.2 Freeware Version. Copyright © Antony Lewis 2003.

www.xulonpress.com

Dedication

Lovingly dedicated to my family:

My husband, Sinclair L. Thorne, II.

My children, Delisa C. Thorne, and James S. Thorne

My mother, Leona D. Cash, and my sister, Linda Reid

My aunts, Evera Dargan, Myrtle Pringle, and Katie Hayward,

and my uncle Robert Pringle

My nieces, Shiretta Rorio, Brenda Reid,

Charlene Reid, Jessica Reid,

and my nephew,

Mark Reid

My children's godmother, Mildred Howard

and her husband, Nicholas Howard,

and my good friend from college, Beryl

Williams

In loving memory of:

My father, James Cash

My sisters, Angelene Carter and Shirley

Johnson

My brothers, James W. Cash, Claude W.

Cash, and Donnie W. Cash

And two very special people who

contributed mightily in my life, Mama Lulu,

and her daughter, Geraldine Jones

Table of Contents

Acknowledgement

I thank you Lord for making this book a reality and for sending those who dedicated their time and effort to its completion.

To my husband, my friend, and my loving supporter Dr. Sinclair L. Thorne, II, thank you so much for your commitment and support you have given me over the years, and with this book. A special thanks to Ms. Deborah E. Willis that has dedicated her time and commitment towards the publication of this book.

I am indebted to my professor, Dr. Edith Anderson, who encouraged me to turn the paper that I wrote for her class into a book, which she believed would help many pastor and minister's wives as they journey with their husband through the task of leading God's people.

I also want to thank First Calvary Missionary Baptist Church Family for all the years of faithful support of the ministry that you have given to me and my husband. I especially want to thank Deaconness Gracie Scott for not thinking it robbery to honor me with a special day, a pastor's wife day, every November.

Thank you Colonel Marilyn Brooks, former Chief of the Department of Nursing, and Rev. Adams, former Chief of Patient Administration at Winn Army

Community Hospital, for your outstanding leadership, that helped me to develop many of the interactional skills I use in my daily contact with people, both in and out of the church.

Foreword

This book was written primarily with the Pastor's wife in mind. There are many wives who are married to Pastors who feel that they have no voice and no way to reach out and ask for help. Very few of us have been trained or taught to be a Pastor's wife. We sort of learn as we go. As a Pastor's wife myself, I have been where you are and this is why I decided to write this book. I want to share with you some of my experiences with my husband, who has been a pastor for 22 years; some lessons that I have learned along this journey; and provide some suggestions that I have picked up along the way that I have found helpful and that may be an encouragement to you, provide you some direction and guidance, and uplift your spirit as you walk the sometimes lonely journey as a Pastor's wife.

This book addresses subjects that you as a Pastors' wife may find beneficial in your daily walk. These subjects include: God's plan for your marriage, how to have healthy communication with your husband, how to develop and apply faith in your relationship with your husband and the congregation, how to possess characteristics that are necessary to be an effective, supportive, and loving Pastor's wife, guidelines that the Pastor's wife should follow if she is to work in the church, how to relate to your children who may be the target of ridicule, hostility, or worse by church members, and other inspirational inserts that may help you along the way. A glossary of terms and a reference list is also provided.

It is my prayer that God will strengthen you as you read this book. Be encouraged and know that you are not alone and by yourself. There are women all over this world who have felt what you are feeling and perhaps some of these women are feeling what you feel right now. Because you may not have a way to find them or to reach out to them, I am reaching out to you through this book. My prayer for is that you will stay the course and find your strength in God, our heavenly father. Do not give up on yourself and definitely do not give up on God. Remember Proverbs 3:5, "Trust in the Lord with all thine heart, and lean not unto thine own understanding. In all thy ways acknowledge him, and he shall direct thy paths" (Proverbs 3:5-6 New King James Version). I know that sometimes this is easier said than done, but you can do all things through Christ who strengthens you (Philippians 4:13).

May God bless you, the Pastor's wife.

Introduction

My husband and I have been friends for 38 years, we have been married for 28 years, and he has been my pastor for 22 years. As a little girl, growing up in Peachland, North Carolina, my dream was to become a secretary, to carry a brief-case to work everyday, and to marry a Hawaiian man. Being a pastor's wife was not something that I had considered as a course for my life. But as I look back over my experiences, I can see how God was pre-paring me for such an office. "A man's heart deviseth his way: but the Lord directeth his steps" (Proverbs 16:9).

My husband was in the military when we met and subsequently married. I had graduated from the University of Fayetteville and I was on my way to New Jersey to interview for a teaching job. But on the way there, while listening to the radio, I heard that a teacher had been pushed out of a window. So instead of going to New Jersey, I made a detour and headed to Washington, DC to spend some time with my sister. I had a degree in Business Education, and I was very good at typing and shorthand. I did not know whether I would get a job in DC, but I decided to trust God and I went by faith to the Pentagon where my sister worked to see if I could get a teaching or administrative position. I applied for several positions, and shortly afterwards, I accepted a job working for the Department of the Nurses Corps. At that time, the Nurses Corps was headed by the first woman General in the United States Army, General Hayes.

As I mentioned, my childhood goals were to become a secretary or an administrative person, to carry a briefcase, and to marry a Hawaiian man. But I also wanted to practice karate. So, some time after arriving in DC, I began karate lessons; and by 1971, three of my four goals had been accomplished; I had a secretary job, I was carrying a briefcase to work, and I was practicing karate.

One day while in karate, I hurt my arm and had to seek medical care. I went to the Forestal Building in DC to have someone look at my arm. The Forestal Building was where the surgeon general worked.

While I was waiting to be seen, I noticed a soldier who was working there and acting like he wanted to wait on me. I really did not want him to wait on me and I was hoping they would send someone else out. Much to my dismay at the time, the persistent soldier was allowed to help me. During the screening, he asked me if I practiced karate, and that was how my husband and I met, and it was the beginning of a long life journey together. And by the way, my husband is not Hawaiian, he is Panamanian.

After being friends for over 10 years, my husband and I were married in November 1981 by the Justice of the Peace and then we had our formal wedding in July 1982 at the Fort Myers Chapel, in Fort Myers, Virginia. My entire hometown of Peachland, North Carolina came to the wedding. I stayed in

DC for twelve years, and worked for the Nurses Corps, the Dental Corps, the Bureau of Engraving and Printing, and the Department of Economics. These jobs helped me to become more patient and helpful, develop administrative and people skills, learn how to resolve conflicts in a healthy manner, and learn how to become a team player with people from diverse backgrounds, nationalities, and socio-economic status. Many people complimented me on being pleasant, personable, and able to get the job done.

My husband was called into the ministry in 1983 in Seoul, Korea. He was, and always has been, serious about the ministry he was called into. We had just come from East Hanover, New Jersey. We came to Hinesville, Georgia, and were told we would be stationed here after the tour in Korea. Before my husband went to Korea, we located a church called St. Luke Missionary Baptist Church. Rev. Alton Jones was the Pastor at that time. There, I met Geri and Mama Lula. These were two of the kindest people I have ever known. Mama Lula took me as her daughter and Geri treated me like her sister. I loved them both. Mama Lula and I would sit in my car for hours just talking about the Lord. Geri and I would go different places praying for others. We spent a lot of family time together eating, singing, and praising God. Another sister, Mildred, became my daughter's, Delisa's godmother later on in our stay. I went over to Korea when my husband was being ordained, but before then, I was alone and the Lord allowed me to the opportunity to study the word and get prepared to do things that I would have to do in the ministry.

I joined my husband in Korea six months after he was there. While in Korea, I taught in the Basic Skills Education Program (BSEP) for the Central Texas College, Korea extension. When we returned to Georgia, after my husband's Korean tour had ended, I continued my employment with Central Texas College at Fort Stewart, and taught marketing and personnel. My goal, however, upon returning to the United States, was to get back into government work; which I eventually was able to do. While at St. Luke Missionary Baptist Church, my husband was relicensed, he was ordained, and he served as an associate minister. I served as a Sunday school teacher. When my husband was called to pastor at

First Calvary Missionary Baptist Church, I joined him there and continued to teach Sunday school to the children and teenagers. This was the beginning of me walking in the calling as a pastor's wife.

My husband was still in the military during the initial years of his pastorate. In fact, while being the pastor of First Calvary Missionary Baptist Church, he was called to deploy in support of Operation Desert Shield/Desert Storm. It was during this time I realized that my individual identity was fading away. I became known, not as Deloise Thorne, but as the First Sergeant's wife and as the Pastor's wife. After we had our children, I was referred to as the mother of Delisa and James. Many times in the ministry, I felt insignificant and overlooked. This used to make me feel pretty bad. It would hurt my feelings and sometimes I would be angry, especially when women would step on my feet to try to get to my husband. Overtime their children and other children began to do the same thing, look over me in their attempt to get to him. I found it very interesting that the men did not run after me like the women ran after my husband. I did not say a lot then and it does not bother me as much now. The last thing that I want to do is embarrass my husband. In all of this, God allowed me to grow spiritually, I prayed and fasted a lot, and the Lord kept me from saying or doing anything that would bring reproach upon my husband, the church, and the ministry.

Whenever you have been married to a man for as long as I have, you have a bond that no one else has, but there will be those who think that they know your husband better than you do. When my husband hurts, I hurt; and whenever someone tries to deceive him, even if he does not act like he is hurt, it affects me. You have to remember that as the pastor's wife, you have a responsibility to share with your husband what you see in the church body, while at the same time, supporting him and not doing anything that would be embarrassing and adversely affect the ministry that God has placed him over.

It is also true that sometimes the pastor becomes so busy trying to keep the congregation content that he forgets about his wife. He attends to his flock and leaves her to handle the affairs of the home. As pastor's wives, we can become unhappy and lose our joy. We have to hang on to the word of God that is proclaimed in Nehemiah 8:10, "The joy of the Lord is our strength." Now, if our strength is weakened, it can allow Satan to get in easier and cause all kinds of chaos and havoc. The best thing for us as Pastor's wives is to pray; pray for the church, our husbands, our families, and pray for ourselves. When 2 Peter 5:7 says, "casting all your cares upon him for he careth for you," it does not mean one thing, but all things. Give God all your cares through prayer.

Everyone likes to be appreciated, and the pastor's wife is often neglected. We are the ones that are usually hurting but cannot show it. When our husbands correct the congregation, we bear the anger from them; and usually if you say anything, they think you are either jealous or you are going through "the change." I am thankful that at First Calvary Missionary Baptist Church, we have a special group of women who have designated a certain time in November of each year to honor me with a banquet. The Deaconness Ministry ensures that I, as the pastor's wife, do not go unnoticed and they honor me not only as the pastor's wife, and not only as my children's mother, but also as an individual with my own unique identity.

I am not the only pastor's wife that has gone through in the ministry and has stayed the course. There are a lot of minister's and pastor's wives that go through different things and I believe as we write about our experiences, we can help each other through the journey. In this book, I have provided some suggestions on how to maintain your spiritual, physical, and emotional strength as you journey with your husband through one of the most difficult jobs in the world, and yet one of the most rewarding. To the pastor's wife, I think it is most important for you to pray, seek God first, and take care of your husband. Ask God to show you what to do. Seek God and ask for direction. Lean not to your own understanding on which way to go. If you take care of your husband, your kids will know that all is well; and then they will be okay. Continue to do the things that you did as an individual before you got married if you can, such as exercise, read, etc., as well as support your husband.

Pastor and minister's wives have a special calling and a special role in the ministry. May God bless you as you handle this office with care, seek God's guidance in all that you do, and work by your husband's side to advance the Kingdom of God.

What is Marriage?

From the very beginning of time, God did not intend for man to be alone. In fact, Genesis records the Lord saying "And the Lord God said, It is not good that the man should be alone; I will make him a help meet for him" (Genesis 2:18). So the Lord put man into a deep sleep and from his rib, he made a woman, who we know as Eve (Genesis 2: 21-23). God's intent for the plan of marriage was that the man and woman would leave their parents and be joined as one (Genesis 2:24). Although many people in the world, in both the past and the present, have been greatly deceived and have altered the course of God's original intent and plan for their marriage, God has not changed and the scripture is still the same. The scripture says that marriage is a covenant with several parts: God brings the woman and the man together; both man and woman are to leave father and mother, be joined together, and become one flesh in physical union. No other relationship, not with the parents or children, is to supersede the bond between husband and wife.

It was God who created marriage, and because God created it, it is holy and it is divine. Marriage and the correct order of marriage are so important to God that he even compares the Church to a marriage.

"Wives, submit yourselves unto your own husbands, as unto the Lord. For the husband is the head of the wife, even as Christ is the head of the church: and he is the savior of the body. Therefore as the church is subject unto Christ, so let the wives be to their own husbands in every thing. Husbands, love your wives, even as Christ also loved the church, and gave himself or it. That he might sanctify and cleanse it with the washing of water by the word. That he might present it to himself a glorious church, not having spot, or wrinkle, or any such thing; but that it should be holy and without blemish. So ought men to love their wives as their own bodies. He that loveth his wife loveth himself. For no man ever yet hated his own flesh; but nourisheth and cherisheth it, even as the Lord the church. For we are members of his body, of his flesh, and of his bones. For this cause shall a man leave his father and mother, and shall be joined unto his wife, and they two shall be one flesh. This is a great mystery: but I speak concerning Christ and the church" (Ephesians 5:22-32).

This is one reason why Satan attacks the marriage, because he knows that God created marriage and that it was designed for man and woman to become as one. Satan does not like unity and oneness.

As pastor's wives, it is imperative that we start our day off with the right priorities: First, pray. "But seek ye first the Kingdom of God and his righteousness, and all these things shall be added to you" (Matthew 6:33). My husband and I are one and we are striving for completeness. I realize that we will be attacked by the enemy quite often. This is why prayer is so important in our lives, so that we may be able to quench those fiery darts that will be thrown at us (Ephesians 6:12-18). We are to support our spouses and keep them lifted up in prayer. We are to watch out for them and encourage them; and if there are some things that you do not like about your spouse, pray about it instead of being confrontational.

The Pastor carries the burden of the congregation that God has placed him over, and in addition to you and the congregation, he needs prayer too (Bruce, n.d.). In Romans 15:30, Paul asked the congregation to pray for him in the name of our Lord Jesus Christ.

In this, the Christian joined Paul in his struggle by praying for him. And Paul requested that this be done, not out of obligation, but because of their love for him that was given to them by the Holy Spirit. Paul's prayer request was that he be rescued from those in Judea who refused to obey God (Romans 15:31). He asked for specific prayer, and we need to pray specific prayers for our Pastors. The Pastor needs prayer for his personal needs, for spiritual wisdom and power, for his family, and for his ministry to the congregation (Bruce). I pray daily for my husband, as my spouse as well as my Pastor. I even pray that whenever someone tries to deceive my husband, be it male or female, that the Holy Spirit will give him the discernment to know that this is not of God.

Remember that God treats the church just like a marriage; therefore, the Pastor has a dual role, he is married to me, his wife, but he is also married to the congregation. Sometimes people ask me, "How do you do it?" And what they are really asking is, "How do you handle your husband being gone so much, being away from the family so much, being at church so much, and helping other people so much, seemingly at the expense of his family?" I just tell them, it is not me. It is the power of the Holy Spirit that keeps me going and allows me to hold things together, not only for the family, but for my husband as well.

Sometimes being married to a Pastor can pose resentment and jealousy from other members of the congregation, but I just pray for those members, especially the females that can truly get out of line.

A husband is to love his wife just as Christ loved the church and gave himself for it (Ephesians 5:25). Wives are to submit to their husbands, as to the Lord. For the husband is head of the wife. The wives are to be subject to their own husbands as is fitting to the Lord (Colossians 3:18). In other words, we are willing to follow his leadership as he follows Christ. Are you willing?

The Importance of Communicating in the Marriage

I feel that some spouses work very well together, as the husband shows his wife that she is number one in his life and that she comes before other women. It is important for the pastor and his wife to sit down together and discusses things of the day. By doing this, they both can find out how they can continue to work to complement the other. This is one way of communicating, working as a team.

Of course there are some pastor-wife teams that just do not work well together. Sometimes in situations like this, the husband acts as if he does not want his wife to know what he is doing. This sets the stage for the wife to begin thinking that he has secrets; which is not good in any relationship, but definitely not in one that God has put together and one that is attempting to advance the Kingdom of God. When the pastor or the pastor's wife has secrets that they keep from each other, they are saying that their spouse is not trustworthy; which can lead to the thought that something is going on either outside the relationship or inside the relationship that may be destructive to their union.

The wife should not have to hear what is going on with her husband from other women nor should the husband with other men. This type of situation will likely cause some difficulty in the relationship and demonstrates a lack of communication. Does this suggest some kind of distrust? We should show some consideration for one another. We as pastor's wives have to convince our spouses that communication is a main ingredient in our marriage. We have to discuss how we feel about different things that happen around us, to us, and within us. And remember, there are times when the husband or wife may offend the other unintentionally, and if this is not addressed, pointing once again to a lack of communication, problems will arise. We as pastors and pastor's wives have to pray and communicate with each other daily.

George (2004) noted several of God's keys to godly speech. These keys are listed below:

1. Soft. "A soft answer turns away wrath, but a harsh word stirs up anger" (Proverbs 15:1 New Century Version). The way we use our words have an affect on our husbands and can cause unnecessary arguments and disagreements.
2. Sweet. "Sweetness of the lips increases learning or influence" (Proverbs 16:21). If you want to get your point across, use pleasant words because they promote instruction and understanding.
3. Suitable. "Pleasant words are like a honey-comb, sweetness to the soul and health to the bones" (Proverbs 16:24). Kind, sweet words

have a medicinal effect on both the body and the soul. Try it.

4. Scant. "In the multitude of words sin is not lacking, but he who restrains his lips is wise" (Proverbs 10:19). The more you talk, the more you are sure to sin! You do not have to reply to everything that is said. Don't talk so much and you will find increased peace and love in your relationships.
5. Slow. "Be swift to hear, slow to speak, slow to wrath" (James 1:19). In even fewer words, make it your aim to listen much, speak little, and do not become angry, "For the wrath of man does not work the righteousness of God" (James 1:20).

You and your spouse may already have an excellent method of communicating and you may communicate often. If so, thank God for such a relationship; because every pastor's wife cannot say the same. For those of you who desire improved communication and increased communication with hour husband, try using some of these techniques listed above. I believe that you will find them helpful and you will find a greater sense of contentment as you journey with your husband down the road of pastoral service.

Is Your Spouse Important To You?

I believe it is very important for us to seek God before we make any decisions in our marriage. When we put God before anything else that we do, whatever we want will be added unto us. The scriptures say, "But seek ye first the kingdom of God and his righteousness; and all these things shall be added unto you" (Matthew 6:33 New King James Version).

It is important that we put our spouses before the children. If the children know that there is stability in the marriage, they will be much more content. And eventually, just as their parents left their mother and father and cleaved unto their mates, God willing, so will our children one day. If you neglect your spouse during the family years, there may be trouble ahead during the empty nest years. If you do not know how to put your spouse before your children, especially if your identity and your sense of worth is tied up in your children, ask the Lord to help you order the relationships in your life as He had planned from the beginning of time; and then trust him to do it.

According to Stephens (2003), there are twenty rules and tools for a great marriage. I have listed a few of those rules: (1) married couples should make a mental list of all the things that would allow their spouses to know that they are priority, even over the children; (2) the husband should tell the wife and vice versa that they are at the top of the list and promise them that they will not let anything push them from that position. Sometimes your spouse will have so many other things on their agenda that they cannot seem to find time to spend with you. Although they may be pressed for time, they need to take the opportunity to spend a few minutes with you; even if you just go to breakfast together one day or just sit and plan things for the future without being interrupted. And by all means, the next time your spouse asks you to do something that would allow the two of you to spend time together, do it without making an excuse or procrastinating.

Because my spouse is important to me, the first thing I do is seek God and ask him to direct and protect my husband daily; and then to give me direction on what I can do to be more loving and more supportive.

Faith is the Key

Faith is the substance of things hoped for and the evidence of things not seen, according to Hebrews 11:1. In other words, this scripture is saying, "You are hoping for something that you cannot see; but you are believing that after you have put faith into action, you will receive what you are believing God for. Faith is not head knowledge. Head knowledge is believing that Jesus exist, but it does not move into the realm of trusting him to do something for you. Faith is also not merely temporary. Temporary faith, for example, is praying for something like traveling, and when you have reached your destination, you no longer need to pray. But faith is trusting in Jesus Christ alone for eternal life. This is the way of survival for the wife of a Pastor.

According to Webster's II New Riverside University Dictionary (1994), survival means the act of surviving, and to survive means to persist through. Pastor's wives and other spouses should be godly at all times and should begin the day with the right priorities. Seek God first because he said in his word that if we seek him first, the other things that we need will be added unto us. A Pastor's wife should be committed to home and family. The ministry will call for a lot of the Pastor's time; therefore, the wife has to be committed to the church, the family, and to serving God through the ministries in the church, and involvement in the community.

Sometimes things will seem difficult, but we must keep the faith that God will take us through any storm that may come. He said if we have faith of a grain of mustard seed, we can move mountains (Matthew 17:20). Faith is a major key to ministry success; and it is the spiritual force through which our ministry for Christ becomes effective (Fackerell, 1996). It is faith in God that brings you what you need to be a godly woman, a supportive wife, a loving mother, and a help to the body of Christ. Where is your faith in God?

How Can the Pastor's Wife Bear the Cross by Having Faith?

As a Pastor's wife, I would expect some trials and persecutions to come in my life and my family's life. Matthew 8:34 (New Century Version) says, "Whoever will come after me, let him deny himself and take up his cross and follow me." So to encourage myself and to encourage other Pastor's wives to hold onto and to develop their faith in God, I have listed some faith-comforting scriptures.

1. Faith brings salvation. (Ephesians 2:8-9) "For by grace are ye saved through faith, not of works, it is the gift of God, not of yourself, lest any man shall boast."
2. Faith brings answers to prayer. (Matthew 21:22). "And whatsoever things you ask in prayer, really believing, you will receive."
3. Faith brings all the benefits of salvation into our lives. This includes healing, prosperity, peace, love, joy, deliverance, and any benefit that the word of God promises us (I Peter 1:8).
4. Faith is a spiritual force through which our ministry for Christ becomes effective; it is a major key to ministry success; and it brings to you what you need for your ministry

(Fackerell, 1996). You may be going through some trials, but you must have faith that God will bring you through. He will not put more on us than what we can bear.

And remember, without faith, we cannot please God (Hebrews 11:6). Are you ready to walk by faith and not by sight?

How Do We Develop Our Faith?

I have listed several of the strategies noted by Fackerell (1996) that pastor's wives can use to develop their faith. These strategies include:

1. Listen to the word of God as much as possible because "Faith comes by hearing, and hearing by the word of God" (Romans 10:17). What we listen to effects what we believe; therefore it is more important to listen to the word of God than to watch a movie or video.

2. God has given all of us a measure of faith, but we have to use it by putting it into action.
3. We must obey God and gain strength as we walk. God will not reveal greater things to us until we are faithful in the things that he has already shown us.
4. Give thanks before you see the results. Do not complain, it will appear that you doubt God. (1 Thessalonians 5:18).
5. Praise and worship the Lord. This helps your faith to grow.
6. Speak the word. By speaking what you believe, you exercise faith. Hear the word and build it into your life. God's word is anointed and has power when it is spoken to change

the spiritual atmosphere (Joshua 1:8; Romans 10:10).

7. Confession of God's word, or saying the same thing as God's word, brings you into the place where the Lord will move to fulfill it.
8. Seek holiness, without which no one will see the Lord. (Hebrews 12:14).
9. Remember to take care of the heart because it is with the heart that man believes (Romans 10:10).

"Through faith also Sara herself received strength to conceive seed, and was delivered of a child when she was past age, because she judged him faithful who had promised. Therefore sprang there even of one, and him as good as dead, so many as the stars of the sky in multitude, and as the sand which is by the sea shore innumerable" (Hebrews 11:11-12 New King James Version).

"And what shall I more say?...Who through faith subdued kingdoms, wrought righteousness, obtained promises, stopped the mouths of lions, Quenched the violence of fire, escaped the edge of the sword, out of weakness were made strong, waxed valiant in fight, turned to flight the armies of the aliens. Women received their dead raised to life again…" (Hebrews11: 32a-35a).

When you stand before the Lord to give an account, will you hear him say, "Well done, thou good and faithful servant; thou hast been faithful over a few things, I will make you ruler over many things: enter thou into the joy of thy Lord" (Matthew 25:21). Today may be the day for you to start developing your faith. Will you accept the call?

Bearing the Cross

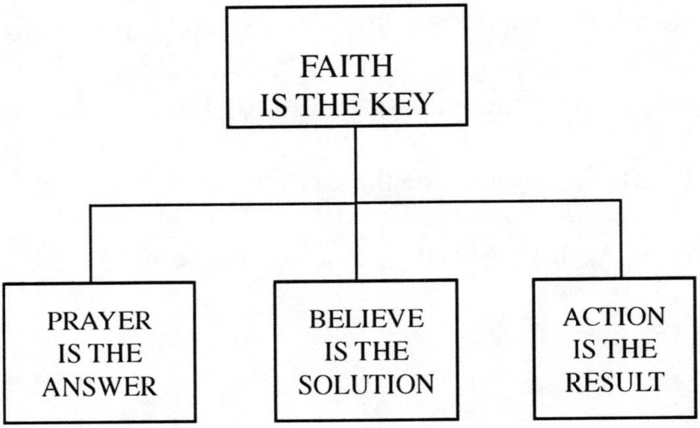

I have included this easy to follow hierarchal chart to show the critical elements of cross-bearing for a pastor's wife. This flowchart can be used by anyone who has decided to take up his cross and follow Christ. "And he said to them all, if any man will come after me, let him deny himself, and take up his cross daily, and follow me" (Luke 9:23).

As pastor's wives, we will be faced with certain unique challenges that will cause us to rest on the bosom of God and cry out to the only One who can keep us from falling, from giving up, from giving in, and from giving out. Develop your faith and build a strong prayer life. Remember what Jesus said, "Man ought always to pray, and not faint" (Luke 18:1b). Believe that God will grant what you ask him for. "And all things, whatsoever ye shall ask in prayer, believing, ye shall receive" (Matthew 21:22). And then follow God's guidance in doing what he would have you to do. "A man's heart deviseth his way: but the Lord directeth his steps" (Proverbs 16:9). Move in the will of God and you too will be able to say, "Nevertheless not my will, but thine be done" (Luke 22:42b). Amen.

You Must Have Good Characteristics to Bear the Cross

A good spouse should be trustworthy and never do anything to bring dishonor to her husband. Your husband should be able to lean and depend on you and seek your advice when everyone else turns their back on him. These are some of the characteristics described of the virtuous woman in Proverbs 31. A pastor should be able to discuss things of a sensitive nature with his wife and be assured that she is not going to take it further.

Like no other person, a pastor's wife has to share her husband with the congregation and many others. I try to be a devoted wife and encourage my husband; listen to whatever he has to discuss with me; and give him support. I honor my husband, respect his work, and encourage him when he delivers his message. I also respect his judgment in church matters because I know that he is following the sovereign God who is in control of all things. Let us not end up like Queen Vashti, in the scriptures. Esther 1:20 says that after Queen Vashti refused to appear before her husband the king, she was banished forever and another queen was chosen. We also do not want to possess the characteristics of Jezebel, who the scriptures report controlled Ahab (I Kings 21:4-7; 14-16). Let us not be a hindrance to the gospel by being a hindrance to our husband.

It is good for the pastor and his wife to take time, get away, and enjoy each other. My husband is my best friend, and we always share things with each other. Of course, he does have some male friends that help to take care of him. But I enjoy the time we spend nurturing each other, even if it is simply going on a ride together to talk, or going to the movies, shopping, exercising, or complimenting each other. My husband is so busy, and because of it, I make it a point to spend as much time with him as possible. We go to the church conventions together; we took a trip to Jerusalem and Germany together. Jerusalem was a great experience for us because my husband got sick while we were on the trip and God performed a wonderful miracle.

My husband was determined to be baptized in the Jordan River, even though the water was very dirty. He was told by some of the people who had gone on the trip with us that God has given man common sense and common sense should tell him that he should not get into the water. But my husband did get into the water. Two of the pastors who went with us, dipped him into the Jordan River and when they brought him out of the water, he was healed. A miracle had happened; his body was completely healed of the sickness that had afflicted him while we were on the trip. The person that spoke of having or not having common sense did not realize that my husband and I walk by faith and not by sight; and that it is faith that brings about healing, not whether the water is clean or dirty. This was the most memorable trip we had together.

I do miss my children when we go on these trips, but I do enjoy spending quality, uninterrupted time with my husband. If you and your husband are finding it difficult to find time together, try getting on his schedule by making an appointment with him to go to lunch or breakfast once or twice a month. I do this, especially when his schedule is very busy and we are pulled two different directions. I look forward to this time every month; and I find these breakfast and lunch meetings to be very filling, leaving us with precious and lasting memories.

Suggested Guidelines for Pastor's Wives

Here is a short list of guidelines that have been suggested by Word (1957) that you can use as a checklist to ensure that you are doing the things necessary to strengthen your personal relationship with your husband, while at the same time, supporting him in the ministry.

1. Be discreet and never discuss with others what your husband has told you in confidence. This could cause confusion among the

other members of the church and your name could come up as having said certain things that bring dishonor and disgrace to yourself, your husband, and the ministry.

2. Stay interested in your husband ministry, this will help you maintain support for what he has been called to do.
3. Be sure to communicate with your husband. Communication is very important in a ministry.
4. Make sure that you give constructive criticism in private, if such recommendations are appropriate.
5. Do not believe everything that someone says about him.

6. Do not be lazy in your work, and serve the Lord joyfully.
7. Make it a point to encourage and compliment your husband often.
8. Pray for your husband in all situations and at all times.
9. Let you husband know that he is special and precious to you.
10. Be devoted to your husband and help him in everyway possible; be his "help meet" (Genesis 2:20).

Before I end this chapter, I want to compare two choices that Moses made with two choices that we have to make as pastor's wives. Moses aligned himself with the Israelites and dedicated his life to the service of the Lord. Will you do the same thing?

Will you align yourself with the people of God and dedicate yourself in complete service for Christ, or will you chose to go your own way and do your own thing at the expense of your relationship with your husband, the church, and ultimately the Lord?

Moses had to make several choices and so do we as pastor's wives

MOSES	PASTOR'S WIFE
1ST Choice Align himself with the Israelites Exodus 2:11-14 Hebrews 11:24-25	Align yourself with the body of Christ Acts 2:38-47
2nd Choice Dedication to God's service Exodus 3:5, 4:18	Dedicate yourself to complete service for Christ Matthew 16:24

Moses made his decisions while standing on Holy ground after being told by God to remove his shoes (Exodus 3:5). When comparing the pastor's wife with Moses, we too have to find ourselves in a place of standing before the Almighty God and deciding whether to become a representative of Christ and do his will, or come up with all kinds of excuses why we cannot follow where he leads. If we decide to follow where the Lord leads, we cannot afford to be negligent or slothful. We have to be diligent in our work as pastor's wives. Romans 12:11 tells us not to be lazy, but to work hard, and serve the Lord with all of our heart. Ephesians 6:10-11 says that we are to put on the whole armor of God so that we may be able to fight against the devil's evil tricks. This scripture makes it very clear that when we are in a fight, it is not against the people of the earth, but it is against rulers and authorities and powers of this world's darkness. It is against spiritual powers of evil in the heavenly world. This is why we have to put on and keep on God's full armor. And if you do this, on that evil day, you will be able to stand strong; and when you have finished the whole fight, you will still be standing (Holy Bible, 1996). What will you do with what you know?

Ten Commandments of a Pastor's Wife

Why did God give Moses the 10 commandments to give to the children of Israel? Because if left to themselves without order or law, they would create chaos and confusion, dishonor God, and destroy themselves. By giving to the people the 10 commandments, God provided his standard of living and interacting, that would be implemented between the people and Him, and between the people themselves.

It is good to have a guide when you do not know where you are going but you need to get to a designated place. Sometimes it is good to have a guide even when you do know where you are going and you know how to get there. A guide simply provides a greater degree of assurance that you will make it to where you want to be. As such, I am providing you with the 10 commandments of a pastor's wife as presented by Word (1957).

I have already discussed much of what is listed in these commandments; and this short list can serve as a summarized reminder of our duties to our God, our husband, our families, our church, our community, and our duty to our self. May God bless you as you follow his will for your life.

The 10 Commandments of a Pastor's Wife

1. Thou shalt not tear down thy husband in public, remembering that one of the cardinal principles of a successful marriage is respect for thy mate's ego.
2. Thou shalt not look disinterested during a service of worship, even though thou has heard this powerful sermon of thy husband for the third time.
3. Thou shalt not accept the presidency of the missionary society, for she who invests herself with office openeth the door of much criticism and robs others of leadership opportunities.
4. Thou shalt not sing in the choir, even if thy voice is operatic quality, unless thou has

the hearty consent of the choir director, the church officers, the staff, and thy husband.

5. Thou shalt not extol thy husband's virtues in public, for his deeds are his best press agent; besides, thou will offend other women who also have perfect husbands.
6. Thou shalt not take unto thyself a confidant, because today's confidant may be tomorrow's adversary. Moreover, confidants always have good memories.
7. Thou shalt not entertain lavishly, dress conspicuously, talk boisterously or lead aggressively – two leaders in a minister's household often wreck the family and disturb an otherwise peaceful flock.

8. Thou shalt not show impatience when the other members of the church are extolled, and thy talents seem small by comparison.
9. Let thy children be restrained by the ideal of being good for goodness sake and not because of public opinion. They are just p.k.'s (pastor's kids), which can be a compliment rather than a gibe.
10. Thou shalt not fail to pray and fill thy days with good works, for the quiet demonstration of God's presence and power in thy daily life may turn more to righteousness than the mighty preaching of thy honored husband. (Above all, let not thy husband suspect this.).

Here is another list of suggestions made by Word (1957) that you may want to consider as you make your way through life as a pastor's wife.

The Pastor's wife shall not gossip:

1. Thou shalt not go up and down as a talebearer among thy people: neither shalt thou stand against the blood of thy neighbor: I am the Lord. (Leviticus 19:16).
2. The words of a talebearer are as wounds, and they go down in the innermost parts of the belly. (Proverbs 18:8).
3. He that goeth about as a talebearer revealeth secrets: therefore meddle not with him that flattereth with his lips (Proverbs 20:19).

4. A talebearer of secrets: but he that is of a faithful spirit concealeth the matter. (Proverbs 11:13).
5. A foreward man soweth strife: and a whisperer separateth chief friends. (Proverbs 16:28).
6. Thy tongue deviseth mischiefs; like a sharp razor, working deceitfully. (Psalms 52:2).
7. The north wind driveth away the rain: so doth an angry countenance a backbiting tongue (Proverbs 25:23).
8. Where no wood is, there the fire goeth out: so where there is no talebearer, the strife ceaseth. As coals are to the burning coals, and wood to the fire; so is a contentious man to kindle strife.

How You Can Bear the Cross in Dealing with Criticism?

As a Pastor's wife, you can expect to have some criticism. I try to accept criticism in a godly manner. It seems that the members of the church, especially the female members, watch what you wear and are always trying to correct something that may be in disarray. I realized early on that if someone is constantly talking about the way I am dressed or talking about how they think things should be done that I am involved in, the only godly alternative thing to do is to thank them for their concern and keep on going.

Sometimes church members can say some very unpleasant things, but God has blessed me with wisdom so that I may discern what is actually happening. Sometimes the devil uses others just to upset us and we must realize that he is also trying to get to the Pastor. He knows that when you get upset it becomes a concern of the Pastor. The word of God lets us know in Philippians 4:13, "I can do all things, through Christ which strengthens me." Although Paul had a thorn in his side, and he asked the Lord three times to remove it, God said unto him, "My grace is sufficient for thee: for my strength is made perfect in weakness. Most gladly therefore will I rather glory in my infirmities that the power of Christ may rest upon me" (2 Corinthians 12:9). He was an example of walking by faith.

I remember someone saying once that a Pastor's wife should stay in her place. I did not quite understand what that meant. I do not play the piano and I do not have a great voice, but I can teach and proclaim the word of God. I believe if God has given me the ability to teach then why should I not be allowed to teach? Genesis 2:18 said "And the Lord said, it is not good that man should be alone; I will make him a help meet for him" (Genesis 2:18). According to Webster's II New Riverside University Dictionary (1994), help means to aid, assist, relieve; and meet means to quality. I believe that I am my husband's help meet, and I can aid and assist in his ministry. Of course, there may be a problem if your husband does not see your capabilities.

Should the Pastor's Wife Work in the Church?

We are all a part of God's plan, and He has a purpose for me as well as for you. A lot of Pastor's wives do not participate or get involved in the activities or functioning of the church because that is the way they were taught. Well, I was not taught to be a Pastor's wife, so I had to do what I knew to do and that was to pray, read the word, and work in the church. I do all that I do to let God know that I appreciate Him sending His only begotten son and giving me salvation, which is free.

I believe if God gives you a gift, you must use it to edify the church. If you do not use what you have, you may lose it. I remember the story in the Bible about the men with the talents. One had five, one had two, and one had one talent. The first two used their talents wisely, while the one with only one talent did not use his; he hid it under a bushel. And his talent was taken away and given to another (Matthew 25:14-30). This parable warns us that our place and service in Heaven will depend on the faithfulness of our lives and service here. A talent represents our abilities, time, resources, and opportunities to serve God while on earth. According to Proverbs 3:5, "Trust in the Lord with all thine heart: and lean not unto thine own understanding. In all thy ways acknowledge him, and he shall direct thy path."

Even though some members do not think that the Pastor's wife should work in the church, they pay close attention to the following concerning the Pastor's wife:

1. They will do things that they know she likes. For example, I was the Director of the Youth Department, which was good because I liked working with the young people. When activities were being planned that involve the youth, I felt that I should have been informed. But there were some in the church who worked with the youth because they knew that was what I liked to do and they would overlooked me. And instead of me directing and providing guidance to the youth, they would do this and then watch to see if I developed a bad

attitude. I stayed humble and gracious and I let the Lord encourage and comfort my heart. You have to do the same.

2. They will notice how many times the Pastor's wife does not come to a service, whether she is sick or not. They will not call to check and see if everything is alright, but they will discuss the fact that she was not present and she should have been there.
3. They like to see her children touch the drums or any other musical instrument because when the instrument is worn or damaged, her child is blamed. They will make sure that she is informed that her child touched this or that and then stand back to see how she will discipline that child.

4. They watch and see who she talks to in the congregation and try to find out what she is talking about. Some will say, "She never speaks to me." But I say, "If I don't speak to you, why don't you speak to me?"
5. They watch and see how often she wears her blue dress; this way they can discuss the fact that she should not wear that dress any more.
6. Some try to find out if her house is clean, or if she can cook, and if she will invite them over to eat. They are not concerned about how long she has been in church that day, how tired she may be, or what may be going on with her and her family.
7. A lot of Pastor's wives know how to play the piano. I am not one of them, but I enjoy

singing. But there are some people who will not want the pastor's wife in the choir. They are afraid that the Minister of Music might let her lead a song.

8. If she mingles with the congregation, some people will avoid speaking to her because she is the Pastor's wife. I remember one time a Deacon said of me, "No one can dislike our Pastor's wife." But I also remember thinking that he might be mistaken because sometimes you will be able to discern certain bad vibes directed towards you.
9. In some churches, members do not want the Pastor's wife to teach Sunday school; but other churches will feel that she should be able to teach.

10. They will bring up situations in the church that they know the Pastor's wife would not agree with just to see if she complains so that they can present this to their group. You have to be very careful about what you say or who you say it to because when you hear it again, it will be a brand new story. That is one reason it is not good to gossip. When it gets back to the Pastor, only your name will be mentioned.

I hear you saying, "If I have to deal with all of this as a Pastor's wife, why would I want to be a Pastor's wife or why should I continue to be a Pastor's wife?" I believe that although we are faced with trouble on every side, the blessings of being a Pastor's wife far exceed the difficulties. Keep your hand in God's hand and he will see you through the tough times. Stay the course!

Are Pastor's Children Really Bad?

I have heard many times that Pastor's children are worse than all other children. I find that to be wrong. The people seem to keep an eye on our children just because my husband is the Pastor. However, there are many times that our children will be blamed for things that they did not do; and the purpose of this is to create confusion not only in your family but also in the church.

It is important that we discipline our children when they are wrong; but not just because they are being blamed by others. A lot of times, other kids as well as their parents will say the Pastor's child did it. But it is important for us as Pastor's wives and mothers to check out the stories that people tell about our kids. I remember on more than one occasion someone talked about my daughter being a Pastor's child in a negative manner. I know that my daughter is very talkative, but just because she is a Pastor's child and she talks a lot was no reason for me to punish her. God has taught her how to be still, be quiet, pray, and wait on the Lord for all that she desires. My daughter truly loves the Lord and will get upset if she thinks someone is misusing the word of God. She is very outspoken and I often remind her that she must listen before she speaks. There is a time for all things.

My son on the other hand, is very quiet and he has experienced being torn down and put down because someone disliked his dad and mom. There was a time when my son would be insulted in front of his class because of what one of his teachers would say about his parents. Can you imagine being mistreated because your parents carry the Word of God?

I prayed that God would give me children and he did. They are a blessing to me and they have filled my life with joy. I pray that you would watch and pray for your children, hold them close to your heart, and pray that God will keep them as they journey with you and your husband through these ministry years.

How Can the Pastor's Wife Be Encouraged While Bearing the Cross?

While doing research on Pastor's wives, I came across some information on a couple, Pastor Harry Shelton Cole and his wife. According to Pastor Cole (n.d.), he and his wife work very well together in the ministry. While implementing a church planting program, Pastor Cole asked his wife to list a particular question that he would ask other pastors, while facilitating discussion on how to improve teamwork between pastors and their spouses. The question asked was, "What is the one thing that you did or wished you had done as pastors to encourage your wife the most in the beginning of your ministry? The following responses were given.

1. Often we push our wives and bring on them burdens that we do not even realize. Example: When the church meets in our apartment, people use the toilet paper that I put on her budget and then she has to ensure that she stays on budget and does not spend too much money the next time she goes shopping. People snoop in her home, which is also her castle, which can leave her feeling very vulnerable and insecure. Be very clear in establishing the boundaries for your people

in order to keep the privacy and sanity of your family intact. Keep your home, your home. Every decision must be made with her approval and if she says no or if she believes someone has gone too far, back her 100%. If you lose a potential member, you still have your wife and ministry. If you lose a wife, you can forget all the potential members because you have no ministry. Love your wife extra special.

2. One wife responded "no matter how busy my husband is, he always has time for me and the children. He has always said, be yourself. His sermons are always an encouragement." Her husband said that his wife has always said she will go with him wherever God is

leading. She has never hesitated when he said that God was leading him to start a church in a far off city or town. She has always been right by his side. I let her know from the very beginning that she was the most important person (next to God) in my life. I have taught many young men that if your wife knows she is number one, you can spend 90% of your time in the ministry and 10% of your time with her, and she will be happy. But if you spend 10% of your time in the ministry, and 90% of your time with your wife, she will be angry while you are out ministering, if she does not know that she is number one.

3. I told my wife that she was my partner in the ministry and that her opinion was very

important to me, and that I wanted to hear it, even though the final decision would have to be mine. A couple we knew taught us the following, "My spouse and I may argue, but we never have a fight; we just sit down and figure out the reason why he is right!"

4. We can go through all the fundamentals of starting a church, the call of God, a place to meet, or even a good sound system, but none is more important than a happy wife and children. One of the first things that we have always done when starting a church was ask the Lord for a good home with more than adequate room, in a nice neighborhood and a good school system for our four boys. Is that asking too much of God? No I don't think so.

He has always provided for our needs and our needs were those three things. If your wife is fearful for her welfare or the safety of her children, you have a problem.

5. One couple who has been married for 50 years stated that there is nothing they can think of that they wished they had known when they first started their ministry because the wife usually told her husband what she wished he knew as soon the issue arose. After so many years together, this wife says of her husband, "When he is away, the house seems too big. When he is home, it is full. He still looks sharp in gray, blue or pink shirts." She instructs, "Communication is to know what to say, and when to say it."

I think there are lessons that can be learned as a result of the experiences of others. At this point in your life, your relationship, and your ministry, what would you like for your spouse to know about you and your needs that you may not have expressed to him or her? Communication is one of the primary keys to having a successful marriage; and lack of communication can definitely destroy what could be a thriving relationship. Stretch out on faith, talk with your spouse, share those things that are near and dear to your heart, and trust God to do the rest.

Pastor's Wife Psalm:

A Morning Prayer for Protection

I have found it a great benefit to get up early in the morning and meet God in my quiet place; in that place of prayer. Most mornings, I go to the church and meet with the other members that have come out for early morning prayer. There are times when I go to early morning prayer and find that I am the only one that is in attendance. I consider this time special time because it allows me to meet with the Lord alone.

Sometimes when I go to pray, I am reminded of scriptures that express to the Lord what it is I want to say. Psalm 5 is such a scripture. This Psalm is a morning prayer where David called out to the Lord. I have a special love for this Psalm. The Psalm is saying, Lord listen to me. I want you to understand what I am saying. Hear my prayer for help because you and you only can I call upon to help me. Lord, every morning you hear my voice. Every morning I tell you what I need and wait for your answer. You are not pleased with the wicked. You do not live with those who do evil. Those people who make fun of you cannot stand before you. You hate evil, you destroy liars, punish those who kill and trick others. Because of your great love, I can come into your Temple. Because I fear and respect you, I can worship in your

Holy Temple. Lord since I have many enemies, show me the right thing to do. Show me clearly how you want me to live. My enemies do not tell the truth; in their hearts they want to destroy others. Their throats are like open graves; they use their tongues for telling lies. God, declare them guilty. Let them fall into their own traps. Send them away because their sins are many; they have turned against you. But let everyone who trusts you be happy; let them sing glad songs forever. Protect those who love you and who are happy because of you. Lord, you bless those who do what is right; you protect them like a soldier's shield.

James 5:16b says, "...The effectual fervent prayer of a righteous man availeth much." Luke 18:1b exhorts, "...that men ought always to pray, and not to faint:" The word men refers to men and women, and boys and girls. Develop your prayer life, and spend quality time with the Lord. "Seek the Lord while he may be found, call upon him while he is near" (Isaiah 55:6). I know that we are busy people and sometimes it is hard to find extra time in the day to pray. But find that time; schedule it in your day if you have to. Remember what Fagerstrom (2006) wrote, "Much prayer, much power; little prayer, little power; no prayer, no power."

The Pastor's Wife

You may sing of your heroes of war and of peace,
Your soldiers of fortune and strife;
When the tumult shall die, and the shouting
shall cease,
Let me sing of the minister's wife.

You may laud to the skies all the learned and wise,
The servants with dignities rife;
My heart says, "Amen," but I take up my pen
In praise of the minister's wife.

Oh, the minister's wife is a cook and a clerk;
A dressmaker, mother, and nurse;
A wonderful teacher, a maid-of-all-work,
And a player and singer, of course!

She must listen, with nerves that are raw to
the quick,
To heartaches and troubles galore;
She must welcome the stranger and visit the sick,
Wearing dresses her sister once wore.

She must work with the aid, and junior HI-Y
She must help with the Sunday school stunts;
Be a leader in missions or tell us all why,
And not miss a prayer meeting once.

She must comfort her husband when
Mondays are blue,
And smooth out his trials – and coats;
Be ready to move every twelve months –
or two
When he shepherds new sheep
(and new goats).

And whether the weather be cloudy or
bright,
In season or out – all the while,
If her heart, be it heavy or light,
She must smile, smile, smile!

Oh, sing of the noble, the great, and the
good,
Whom you meet in the course of your life;
I take up the strain, be it here understood
In praise of the pastor's wife.

Anonymous

If you have never heard it before, let me be the first to say that you, the Pastor's wife, are a very special person whom God has placed beside a very special man that God has charged to lead a very special people. 2 Thessalonians 3:13 admonishes us, "But ye, brethren, be not weary in well doing." Stay the course and do not give up. Do not give up on yourself, your husband, your family, the church, or the Lord. Paul goes a little farther in Galatians when he says, "And let us not be weary in well doing: for in due season we shall reap, if we faint not" (Galatians 6:9). Just like Paul, we too want to be able to say in that final day, "I have fought a good fight, I have finished my course, I have kept the faith: Henceforth there is laid up for me a crown of righteousness, which the Lord, the righteous judge, shall give me at that day: and not to me only, but unto all them also that love his appearing" (II Timothy, 4:7-8).

Summary

Pastor's wives are unique people with unique challenges that are faced by very few others. Our husbands are always on call, and as a result, we are always sharing them with other people. Although we understand and appreciate the importance of the ministry God has given them, we confess that we often feel forgotten, neglected, and invisible; not only by the people of God, but also by our husbands. Hosea 4:6 says "My people are destroyed for lack of knowledge." I have written this book with the intent of providing you with knowledge, or strategies and recommendations that you can use to bind you and your husband closer together, not only as a ministry team, but as husband and wife.

It is imperative that we deny ourselves, pick up the cross, and follow Jesus. It takes a lot of prayer and faith to bear the cross of a Pastor's wife, daily. But remember, Jesus prayed as he healed the sick; he prayed as he fed the hungry; he prayed as he raised the dead; he prayed for his disciples; he prayed for himself; and he prayed for us. Yes, he prayed for you and for me. At the last supper, he prayed that all those who might believe on him would be one. Jesus is the best gift that has ever been given to us, and he lived a life of prayer. So what about us? If Jesus had to pray and he is our role model, so we should also pray.

We cannot do anything on our own. "...Not by might, nor by power, but by my spirit, saith the Lord of hosts" (Zechariah 4:6). This work, this ministry, our service and support for our husbands and God's people, is not about us, but about God. We must have faith and believe that God is who He says he is and that he will do what he said he would do. "But he that shall endure unto the end, the same shall be saved" (Matthew 24:13).

As Pastor's wives, we must read the word for ourselves so that we may grow. "Study to shew thyself approved unto God, a workman that needeth not to be ashamed, rightly dividing the word of truth" (II Timothy 2:15). The story about Martha and Mary is a good example. Martha insisted on serving rather than listening to the word. But Mary knew the importance of getting close to Jesus and learning of Him (Luke 10:38-42). We too have to learn to get closer to the Father by studying and meditating on the word of God. We have to learn to trust Him. Sometime we will ask the Father for something, and take it to the altar. But instead of trusting God and leaving our problems at the altar, we bring them back with us. The Apostle Peter had an answer to this. He says, "Humble yourselves therefore under the mighty hand of God, that he may exalt you in due time: Casting all your care upon him; for he careth for you" (I Peter 5:6-7). Does God care? Yes he does!

God has also told us to put on the whole armor of God so that we may stand against the wiles of the devil, not only as Pastor's wives, but Christians as well (Ephesians 6:11). We are all in a spiritual warfare at one time or another, therefore it is imperative for you to be cognizant of who you are fighting. "For we wrestle not against flesh and blood, but against principalities, against powers, against rulers of the darkness of this world, against spiritual wickedness in high places" (Ephesians 6:12). So when conflict comes at you from within the church, it is spiritual warfare. When conflict comes at you from outside the church, it is spiritual warfare. When conflict comes at your family and tries to tear it apart at the very foundation, remember it is spiritual warfare; and you are not helpless in this fight. Prayer, faith, believing, and action all work together to bring about victory after victory.

Do not give up on yourself, your husband, your family, your church, or God. Trust in the Lord with all thine heart; and lean not unto thine own understanding. In all thy ways acknowledge him, and he shall direct thy paths. Be not wise in thine own eyes: fear the Lord, and depart from evil. It shall be health to thy navel, and marrow to thy bones" (Proverbs 3: 5-8). Hold onto the word of God for you will truly find it to be a great source of comfort. "Thy word is a lamp unto my feet, and a light unto my path" (Psalm 119:105).

As a child, I may not have dreamed of becoming a Pastor's wife; but after 22 years of serving by my husband's side, I would not trade it for the world. I love my husband dearly, and I stand by his side because I know that he is following Christ. He makes time for the family, and we make time for us. After

28 years of marriage, we are still best friends; and to God be the glory.

Yes, there is a cross to bear as a Pastor's wife. And if he has chosen you to bear it, be honored, and be humbled. For you are numbered with his Son whom he allowed to bear the cross up Mt. Calvary, to be crucified on that old rugged cross, to be taken down from the cross and placed in a borrowed tomb, and then to raise him up early on the third day. "It is a faithful saying: For if we be dead with him, we shall also live with him: If we suffer, we shall also reign with him..."(II Timothy 2:11-12a). Do not quit before you have finished your course. Perhaps this book will give you the courage to reach out to other Pastor's wives that you trust, and receive courage and support from them.

If you are at peace in your relationship with your husband, your children, and the people of God, perhaps you too have found the word of God to be true, "...for the joy of the Lord is your strength" (Nehemiah 8:10). There is a cross to bear as a Pastor's wife; but if you can bear through the pain, on the other side is joy. And that joy can be found in this life and the one to come. May the Lord bless you and keep you is our prayer.

About the Author

Mrs. Deloise C. Thorne, a native of Peachland, North Carolina, was born November 13, 2948. She is married to Rev. Dr. Sinclair L. Thorne. She has two children: Delisa C., and James S. Thorne; and two step-children: Deyanira D., and Sinclair L. Thorne, III.

Mrs. Thorne's educational background includes: graduating from East Polkton High School in Peachland, North Carolina; graduating from Fayetteville State University in Fayetteville, North

Carolina, with a Bachelor of Science Degree in Business Education; and graduating from Trinity School of Religion in Hinesville, Georgia with a Doctorate in Counseling and Christian Education.

She is retired after 30 years of Federal Government service; having worked in New Jersey and Savannah, Georgia for the Internal Revenue Service; In Washington, D.C. for the United States Army Nurses Corp, the United States Army Dental Corp, the Bureau of Engraving and Printing, and the Department of Economics. At Fort Stewart, Georgia, she worked at the Winn Army Community Hospital in the Department of Patient Administration and subsequently for the Deputy Commander of Administration, and for the Chief of the Department of Nursing. She worked part-time as an instructor for the Basic Skills Education Program (BSEP) at Central Texas College in Korea and at Fort Stewart, Georgia; and she is currently substituting as a teacher for the Liberty County Board of Education in Hinesville, Georgia.

She faithfully serves the First Calvary Missionary Baptist Church under the leadership of her husband, Pastor Sinclair L. Thorne as a Sunday school teacher, teacher for Youth Evangelism Explosion, Coordinator for the Tutoring program, choir member, Missionary Ministry instructor and Program Coordinator, and President of the Minister's Spouse's Ministry.

She also currently serves as the Youth Director for the Ludowici District of the Tattnall Baptist Association in Southern Georgia; the Secretary and the Coordinator for the Women of Excellence of the First District of the Georgia Missionary Baptist Convention; and the Dean of the Tattnall Baptist Association, Congress of Christian Education.

Glossary

Bear – to suffer, endure, abide, tolerate, to put up with something trying or painful.

Benefit – something that promotes well-being

Characteristics – a special quality or identity

Commandment – the act of commanding

Communication – a process by which information is exchanged.

Criticism – the act of criticizing.

Cross – an affliction that tries one's virtue, steadfastness, or patience.

Develop – expand by a process of growth

Faith – the substance of things hoped for, the evidence of things not seen.

Marriage – an institution whereby a man and a woman are joined together by Holy matrimony.

Wife – a female partner in a marriage.

All definitions are taken from the New Century Version Holy Bible (1996).

References

Bruce, W. (n.d.). Praying for Christian leaders: Pastor's need prayer too. Retrieved from http://www.liftupusa.com/pnpt.html

Cole, H. (n.d.). Encouraging your wife. Retrieved from http://www.baptistchurchplanting.com/bcpachive.

Fackerell, M. (1996). Testimony of Michael Fackerell. Retrieved from http://www.christian-faith.com/html/page/testimony-of-michael-fackerell.

Fagerstrom, D.L. (2006). The ministry staff member: A contemporary, practical handbook to equip, encourage, and empower. Grand Rapids, MI: Zondervan

George, E. (2004). Wife after God's own heart. Eugene, OR: Harvest Publishers.

Green, J.B. (1996). New Century Version Holy Bible, Forth Worth, TX: Word Publishing.

Holy Bible, New King James Version, (1988). Indianapolis, IN: B.B. Kirkbride Bible Co.

Stephens, S. (2003). 20 rules and tools for a great marriage. Wheaton, IL: Tyndale House Publishers

The pastor's wife (n.d.). Anonymous.

Webster's II New Riverside University Dictionary (1994). Boston, MA: The Riverside Publishing Company.

Word, F. (1957). Northwest College of Bible. Portland, OR.

LaVergne, TN USA
17 September 2010
197415LV00001B/30/P

9 781609 574680